THIS WALKER BOOK BELONGS TO:

_____

_____

_____

_____

Monster Maths books aim to teach basic
mathematical concepts in an entertaining way.
In this book, the game is to compare the left and
right-hand pictures on each page and pick out
and talk about the differences between them.
Learning to make simple comparisons is one of the
first steps towards understanding measurement.

The books in this series were produced with
the help of the Pre-school Playgroups Association
and with advice from parents, teachers and
children. The publishers thank them all.

First published 1984 by Walker Books Ltd
87 Vauxhall Walk, London SE11 5HJ

This edition published 1988
Reprinted 1989
© 1984, 1988 Walker Books Ltd

Printed in Hong Kong by
Sheck Wah Tong Printing Press Ltd

British Library Cataloguing in Publication Data
Satchwell, John
Big and little. – (Monster maths)
1. Mathematics   Juvenile literature
I. Title   II. Sleight, Katy   III. Series
510   QA40.5
ISBN 0-7445-1079-1

Big and Little

by John Satchwell
Illustrated by Katy Sleight

WALKER BOOKS
LONDON

Today the monster
is going on holiday.

tight

loose

long

short

big

little

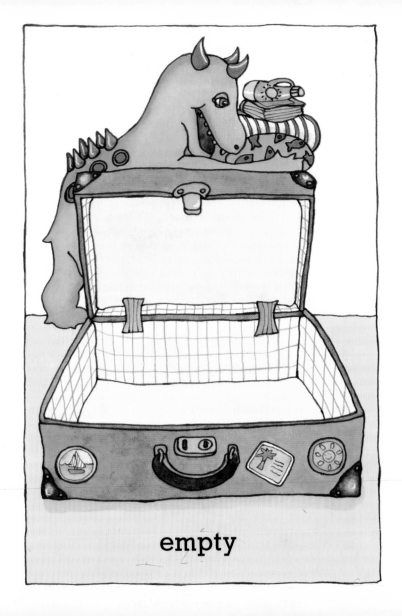

empty

full

top

bottom

down

wet

dry

fast

slow

hard

soft

thick

thin

awake

asleep

MORE WALKER PAPERBACKS

FIRST READERS

Colin & Jacqui Hawkins
TERRIBLE, TERRIBLE TIGER

Chris Riddell
BEN AND THE BEAR

Allan Ahlberg
& Colin McNaughton
Red Nose Readers

MAKE A FACE	SO CAN I
BIG BAD PIG	BEAR'S BIRTHDAY
SHIRLEY'S SHOPS	PUSH THE DOG
TELL US A STORY	ONE, TWO, FLEA!

Colin West
'HAVE YOU SEEN THE CROCODILE?'

Sally Grindley & Clive Scruton
FOUR BLACK PUPPIES

Sarah Hayes & Helen Craig
THIS IS THE BEAR